- Before cooking food, preheat the fat or oil until a faint haze rises from it, but take care not to let it get so hot it smokes. If the oil fails to reach a certain temperature before adding food, it will be absorbed by the food, making the food soggy.

Deep-frying

- Most oils are suited to deep-frying – read labels to check this – and some solid types of shortening can also be used.
- The pan you use for deep-frying should be slightly over half-full of oil; excessive oil can be dangerous.
- When oil is hot enough, it will be still, with a slight haze (not smoke) rising from the surface. Drop a cube of bread into the oil if in doubt; if the oil is ready, the bread should sink to the bottom, then rise to the surface almost immediately and turn golden brown.

4 crisp little potato

rösti with lemon chive cream

3 medium potatoes (600g)
20g butter
1 medium white onion (150g), chopped finely
20g butter, extra

lemon chive cream
90g packaged cream cheese
2 tablespoons sour cream
1 teaspoon grated lemon rind
1 tablespoon lemon juice
1 tablespoon finely chopped fresh chives

Grate potatoes coarsely; using absorbent paper, squeeze excess liquid from potato.
Heat butter in large non-stick frying pan, add onion; cook, stirring, until onion is soft. Add potato, stir until potato is sticky; cool slightly.
Shape level teaspoons of potato mixture into rounds with wet fingers; flatten slightly. Heat extra butter in same pan; cook rösti until browned on both sides, drain on absorbent paper. Serve warm, topped with lemon chive cream, and extra chives and dill, if desired.
Lemon chive cream Beat cheese and sour cream in small bowl with wooden spoon until smooth; add rind, juice and chives.

MAKES 40
per rösti 2g fat; 105kJ
on the table in 40 minutes

contents

British & North American Readers:
Please note that Australian cup and
spoon measurements are metric. A quick
conversion guide appears on page 63.
A glossary explaining unfamiliar terms
and ingredients begins on page 60.

2 the secret's out

These tips will help you cook burgers, rösti and fritters to perfection – they'll be golden and crispy, they'll hold together and they'll be cooked through.

Crumby preparation

Breadcrumbs are a common inclusion in burgers and fritters – they act as a binding agent, ensuring the burger or fritter keeps its shape during the cooking process.

Stale breadcrumbs

Often called soft breadcrumbs, these crumbs can be made at home. Simply remove crusts from one- or two-day-old bread, break bread into pieces, place pieces in a blender or food processor then blend or process until fine. Store any leftover crumbs in sealed plastic bags in the freezer for later use.

Packaged breadcrumbs

Often called dry breadcrumbs, these are used to create a crisp coating on burgers and fritters, and can be obtained at the supermarket or made at home. Place slices of one- or two-day-old bread on baking trays; cook in the oven, at the lowest temperature setting, for several hours or until slices are crisp and pale brown. Cool bread, break into pieces, place pieces in a blender or food processor then blend or process until fine.

Perfect patties

- When making patties, the higher the fat content of the minced meat, the more patties shrink during cooking. Make patties larger than the bun they are to be served on to allow for shrinkage.
- Don't overmix the ingredients; the resultant mixture will be heavy and dense.
- Dampen your hands when shaping patties so the meat won't stick to your fingers.
- If you intend freezing hamburger patties (raw or cooked), first separate them with squares of plastic wrap. This will ensure the patties are easy to pry apart and defrost as needed.

Let's fry away

Shallow-frying

- Burgers, rösti and fritters that are to be shallow-fried require you to use enough oil that it comes halfway up the sides of the food.
- Most oils are suitable for shallow-frying, as is ghee (clarified butter), but butter is not, as it is prone to burning. Butter can, however, be used successfully in combination with oil. Low-fat spreads cannot be used to shallow-fry as they contain a high proportion of water.

6 fish burger

600g boneless white fish fillets, chopped

1 egg

1/4 teaspoon sweet paprika

1 teaspoon ground cumin

1 teaspoon ground coriander

1/2 teaspoon garlic salt

1 loaf pide

2 lebanese cucumbers (260g)

3/4 cup (210g) yogurt

1 tablespoon finely chopped fresh mint

Blend or process fish, egg, spices and garlic salt until smooth. Using hands, shape mixture into four patties. Cook patties in large heated oiled non-stick frying pan until browned both sides and cooked through.
Cut pide into four even pieces; slice horizontally through the centre of each piece. Toast pieces, cut-side up, under heated grill.
Using a vegetable peeler, slice cucumbers into thin strips.
Combine yogurt and mint in small bowl.
Top pide bases with patties, cucumber and yogurt mixture, then remaining pide.

SERVES 4
per serving 9.6g fat; 2211kJ
on the table in 35 minutes

salmon patties with

corn and avocado salsa

1 cup (200g) medium-grain white rice

415g can red salmon, drained, flaked

2 green onions, chopped finely

1 egg, beaten lightly

corn and avocado salsa

1 fresh corn cob (250g)

2 medium tomatoes (380g), seeded, chopped finely

1 medium avocado (250g), chopped finely

1 tablespoon drained, pickled, sliced jalapeño chillies, chopped finely

1 tablespoon finely chopped fresh coriander

2 tablespoons lime juice

1 tablespoon peanut oil

Cook rice in large saucepan of boiling water until just tender; drain. Rinse rice under cold water; drain well. Combine rice, salmon, onion and egg in large bowl. Using hands, shape 1/3-cup measures of mixture into patties.

Cook patties, in batches, in large heated oiled non-stick frying pan until browned both sides and heated through. Serve patties with corn and avocado salsa.

Corn and avocado salsa Heat medium oiled non-stick frying pan, add corn; cook until browned and cooked through. Cut kernels from cob. Combine corn and remaining ingredients in medium bowl.

SERVES 4
per serving 26.7g fat; 2276kJ
on the table in 35 minutes

8 pork burgers

500g minced pork

1 cup (70g) stale breadcrumbs

1 egg, beaten lightly

1 medium brown onion (150g),
chopped finely

2 cloves garlic, crushed

2 tablespoons finely chopped fresh mint

2 tablespoons finely chopped
fresh coriander

2 teaspoons worcestershire sauce

1 tablespoon tomato sauce

1 loaf pide, cut into 6 pieces

½ cup (130g) prepared hummus

80g prepared tabbouleh

6 small pieces bottled roasted
capsicum (80g)

Combine pork, breadcrumbs, egg,
onion, garlic, herbs and sauces. Using
hands, shape mixture into six patties.
Grill or barbecue patties until browned
both sides and cooked through.
Split pide pieces in half; grill or
barbecue until lightly browned.
Spread bases with hummus, top
with patties, tabbouleh and capsicum,
then remaining bread halves.

SERVES 6
per serving 14.8g fat; 1927kJ
on the table in 35 minutes

10 super **beef** burgers

500g minced beef

1 medium white onion (150g), grated

1/4 cup (25g) stale breadcrumbs

vegetable oil, for shallow-frying

2 medium white onions (300g), sliced thinly

4 small dampers

4 cheese slices

2 medium tomatoes (300g), sliced thinly

125g alfalfa sprouts

225g can sliced beetroot, drained

175g watercress

barbecue sauce

1/2 cup (125ml) tomato sauce

1 small red capsicum (150g), chopped finely

1 tablespoon worcestershire sauce

1/4 teaspoon chilli powder

Combine beef, grated onion and breadcrumbs in large bowl. Using hands, shape mixture into four patties.

Heat oil in large frying pan; cook patties and sliced onion, turning patties occasionally, until onion is soft and patties are cooked through. Drain on absorbent paper.

Split dampers; fill with barbecue sauce, onion, patties, cheese, tomato, sprouts, beetroot and watercress.

Barbecue sauce Combine ingredients in medium bowl.

SERVES 4
per serving 38.2g fat; 3102kJ
on the table in 35 minutes

rissoles with
tomato sauce

750g minced beef

1 cup (70g) stale
breadcrumbs

1/3 cup (25g) grated
parmesan cheese

1 clove garlic, crushed

2 tablespoons finely
chopped fresh
flat-leaf parsley

2 tablespoons finely
chopped fresh basil

1 egg, beaten lightly

tomato sauce

1 1/2 cups (375ml)
bottled pasta sauce

1 small red capsicum
(150g), sliced thinly

1 tablespoon coarsely
chopped fresh basil

Combine beef, breadcrumbs, cheese, garlic,
herbs and egg in large bowl. Using floured
hands, shape mixture into 12 rissoles.
Heat large oiled non-stick frying pan; cook
rissoles until browned both sides and cooked
through. Serve with tomato sauce; accompany
with kumara mash, if desired.
Tomato sauce Combine ingredients in medium
saucepan; stir over heat until sauce boils.

SERVES 4
per serving 22.1g fat; 1941kJ
on the table in 35 minutes

12 thai fish cakes

with noodle salad

Redfish, usually sold skinned as fillets, is ideal for these fish cakes because of its delicate flavour. You can, however, use practically any mild-flavoured, skinless fish fillet.

2/3 cup loosely packed fresh coriander leaves

1/2 cup loosely packed fresh mint leaves

4 red thai chillies, quartered, seeded

600g firm white fish fillets, chopped coarsely

1 clove garlic, crushed

1 egg white

250g rice vermicelli

2 teaspoons sugar

1/4 cup (60ml) lime juice

1 tablespoon sambal oelek

1 lebanese cucumber (130g), seeded, chopped finely

100g snow peas, sliced thinly

Blend or process half of the coriander, half of the mint, half of the chilli, fish, garlic and egg white until mixture forms a paste; using hands, shape mixture into 12 patties.

Cook patties, in batches, in heated large non-stick frying pan until browned both sides and cooked through.

Place noodles in large heatproof bowl; cover with boiling water. Stand noodles until just tender; drain, keep warm.

Meanwhile, combine sugar, juice and sambal oelek in small saucepan; bring to a boil.

Chop remaining coriander, mint and chilli finely. Place in large bowl with noodles, sambal mixture, cucumber and snow peas; toss to combine. Serve fish cakes on noodle salad.

SERVES 4
per serving 5.1g fat; 1566kJ
on the table in 30 minutes

14 **prawn** cakes
with choy sum

1.25kg uncooked prawns, peeled, deveined

2 tablespoons grated fresh ginger

2 red thai chillies, seeded, chopped finely

2 teaspoons finely grated lime rind

2 tablespoons peanut oil

500g choy sum, trimmed

1/3 cup (80ml) sweet chilli sauce

2 tablespoons soy sauce

Blend or process prawns, ginger, chilli and rind until well combined. Using hands, shape mixture into eight patties.

Heat oil in large non-stick frying pan; cook patties until browned both sides and cooked through.

Meanwhile, boil, steam or microwave choy sum until just wilted; drain well.

Serve prawn cakes with choy sum and combined chilli and soy sauce.

SERVES 4
per serving 11g fat; 1098kJ
on the table in 35 minutes

soy patties with herb yogurt

1 tablespoon olive oil

1 medium red onion (170g), chopped finely

2 cloves garlic, crushed

1 medium red capsicum (200g), chopped finely

3 cups (210g) stale breadcrumbs

2 x 300g cans soy beans, rinsed, drained

2 eggs, beaten lightly

1/2 cup chopped fresh flat-leaf parsley

2 teaspoons grated lemon rind

3/4 cup (60g) grated parmesan cheese

1/3 cup (50g) pine nuts, toasted

herb yogurt

3/4 cup (210g) yogurt

1 clove garlic, crushed

1 tablespoon lemon juice

2 tablespoons chopped fresh flat-leaf parsley

2 tablespoons chopped fresh chives

Heat oil in medium frying pan; cook onion, garlic and capsicum, stirring, until onion is soft. Preheat oven to hot. Process breadcrumbs, beans, egg, parsley, rind, half of cheese, and onion mixture until combined; stir in pine nuts. Using hands, shape 1/3-cup measures of mixture into patties, place on oven tray; top with remaining cheese.
Bake in hot oven, turning once halfway through cooking time, for 20 minutes or until browned. Serve with herb yogurt.
Herb yogurt Combine ingredients in small bowl.

SERVES 4
per serving 30.3g fat; 2433kJ
on the table in 45 minutes

crispy
pumpkin
rösti

You will need a 300g piece
of pumpkin for this recipe.

1¹/₂ cups finely grated pumpkin

1 egg, beaten lightly

*2 tablespoons finely chopped
fresh flat-leaf parsley*

*¹/₄ cup (20g) grated
parmesan cheese*

¹/₄ cup (35g) plain flour

60g butter

Combine pumpkin, egg, parsley,
cheese and flour in medium bowl.
Heat butter in large non-stick
frying pan; cook ¹/₄-cup measures
of pumpkin mixture until
browned both sides.

SERVES 2
per serving 31g fat; 1494kJ
on the table in 30 minutes

18 lamb and **fetta** rissoles

400g minced lamb

1 small brown onion (80g), chopped finely

1 clove garlic, crushed

1/3 cup (40g) seeded black olives, chopped finely

60g fetta cheese, crumbled

1/2 cup (35g) stale breadcrumbs

1 egg white

Combine ingredients in medium bowl; using hands, shape mixture into eight rissoles. **Heat** large oiled non-stick frying pan; cook rissoles until browned both sides and cooked through. **Serve** with tomato relish, if desired.

SERVES 4
per serving
13.6g fat; 1108kJ
on the table in
20 minutes

fennel fritters

1 tablespoon finely chopped fresh fennel

1 medium fennel bulb (500g), chopped finely

3 green onions, chopped finely

1 small carrot (70g), grated

2 bacon rashers, chopped finely

2 eggs, beaten lightly

75g ricotta cheese

1/4 cup (35g) plain flour

2 teaspoons baking powder

vegetable oil, for shallow-frying

Combine fennel, fennel bulb, onion, carrot, bacon, egg, cheese, flour and baking powder in medium bowl.
Shallow-fry heaped tablespoons of mixture in hot oil until golden brown and cooked through; flatten slightly during cooking. Drain on absorbent paper.

SERVES 4
per serving 29.6g fat; 1468kJ
on the table in 30 minutes

20 middle-eastern
lamb burger

1 tablespoon olive oil

1 medium white onion
(150g), chopped finely

2 cloves garlic, crushed

1 teaspoon ground ginger

1 teaspoon ground
coriander

1 teaspoon ground cumin

2 tablespoons
dried currants

2 tablespoons finely
chopped fresh coriander

500g minced lamb

1 tablespoon sambal oelek

1/2 cup (35g) stale
breadcrumbs

1 medium red
capsicum (200g)

2 baby eggplants (120g)

4 wholemeal bread rolls

50g baby rocket leaves

yogurt sauce

1 cup (280g) yogurt

1 lebanese cucumber
(130g), seeded, chopped

2 tablespoons finely
chopped fresh mint

1 clove garlic, crushed

Heat oil in medium frying pan; cook onion and garlic, stirring, until onion is soft. Add spices, stir until fragrant.
Combine onion mixture, currants, fresh coriander, lamb, sambal oelek and breadcrumbs in medium bowl; using hands, shape mixture into four patties. Cook patties on heated oiled grill plate (or grill or barbecue) until browned both sides and cooked through.
Meanwhile, cut capsicum into four flat pieces and eggplants into thin slices lengthways. Barbecue or grill vegetables on each side until lightly browned and softened. Peel skin from capsicum.
Cut rolls in half. Grill cut sides until toasted. To assemble burgers, top roll bases with capsicum, eggplant, patties and rocket. Serve with roll tops and yogurt sauce.
Yogurt sauce Combine ingredients in medium bowl.

SERVES 4
per serving 22.1g fat; 2215kJ
on the table in 50 minutes

22 saffron scrambled eggs on
corn cakes

1 fresh corn
cob (250g)

¾ cup (105g)
plain flour

1 teaspoon
sweet paprika

1 tablespoon
finely chopped
fresh coriander

¼ cup (60ml) milk

3 egg whites

1 egg

1 egg white, extra

pinch saffron threads

Cut corn kernels from cob. Combine corn, flour, paprika and
coriander in medium bowl; stir in milk, mix until combined.
Beat egg whites in small bowl with electric mixer until soft peaks
form; fold egg whites into corn mixture. Cook ¼-cup measures of
corn mixture in heated oiled large non-stick frying pan until browned
both sides and cooked through.
Combine egg, extra egg white and saffron in medium bowl; beat
lightly with a fork. Cook egg mixture in lightly oiled non-stick frying
pan, stirring gently, until creamy and just set. Serve scrambled
eggs with corn cakes.

SERVES 4
per serving 2.8g fat; 750kJ
on the table in 40 minutess

rösti

**4 medium
potatoes (800g)**

**salt and freshly ground
black pepper**

60g butter

Cook potatoes in large saucepan of boiling water
until just tender; drain. Cool then peel potatoes.
(Cover and refrigerate overnight, if possible).
Grate potato; add salt and pepper to taste.
Heat half of the butter in large frying pan, add
potato; flatten to form thin layer. Cook about
15 minutes or until golden brown on underside.
Place a large plate over pan; invert rösti onto it.
Heat remaining butter in pan, slide rösti into pan;
cook for 15 minutes or until other side is golden.
Cut into wedges; serve with salad, sour cream,
green onion and smoked salmon, if desired.

SERVES 4
per serving 12.5g fat; 926kJ
on the table in 45 minutes

24 fish patties with
sweet chilli-coriander sauce

1 small carrot (70g), grated

1 small zucchini (90g), grated

3 green onions, chopped

2 cloves garlic, quartered

1 red thai chilli, seeded, chopped

2 teaspoons grated fresh ginger

1 tablespoon chopped
fresh coriander

1 teaspoon grated lime rind

375g boneless white fish
fillets, chopped

1 tablespoon fish sauce

2/3 cup (100g) plain flour

1 teaspoon ground turmeric

1/4 cup (60ml) peanut oil

sweet chilli-coriander sauce

1/2 cup (125ml) white vinegar

1 1/2 tablespoons brown sugar

2 red thai chillies, seeded,
chopped finely

1 teaspoon cornflour

1/4 cup (60ml) water

1 tablespoon finely chopped
fresh basil

2 teaspoons finely chopped
fresh coriander

Blend or process carrot, zucchini, onion, garlic, chilli, ginger, coriander and rind until finely chopped. Add fish and sauce; blend or process until well combined.

Toss level tablespoons of fish mixture in combined flour and turmeric; shape into patties.

Heat oil in large non-stick frying pan; cook patties, over medium heat, until lightly browned both sides and cooked through. Remove from pan; drain on absorbent paper. Serve with sweet chilli-coriander sauce.

Sweet chilli-coriander sauce Combine vinegar, sugar and chilli in small saucepan; stir over medium heat until sugar is dissolved. Blend cornflour with the water; stir into vinegar mixture, over medium heat, until sauce boils and thickens slightly. Remove from heat; stir in herbs.

SERVES 4

per serving 18g fat; 1555kJ

tip For easier handling, refrigerate patties for 15 minutes before cooking.

on the table in 40 minutes

26 red curry
noodle cakes

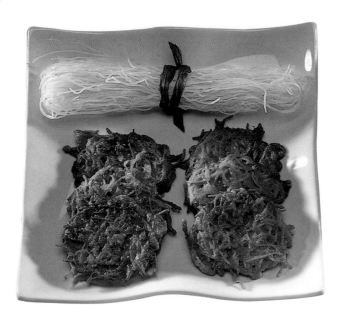

80g dried rice
vermicelli

2 green onions,
chopped finely

1/2 cup (75g) plain flour

2 eggs, lightly beaten

1/4 cup (60ml)
coconut milk

1/4 cup (75g) red
curry paste

peanut oil, for
shallow-frying

Place noodles in small heatproof bowl,
cover with boiling water; stand until just
tender, drain. Cut noodles into 5cm lengths.
Combine noodles, onion, flour, egg, coconut
milk and curry paste in medium bowl.
Cook level tablespoons of mixture, in batches,
in hot oil until browned and cooked through;
drain on absorbent paper.

MAKES 18
per cake 5.8g fat; 353kJ
on the table in 30 minutes

patties with sweet chilli sauce

500g chicken thigh fillets, chopped

1 medium red capsicum (200g), chopped

2 cloves garlic, quartered

1/2 cup firmly packed fresh coriander leaves

2 red thai chillies, seeded, chopped

1 tablespoon fish sauce

1 egg

1 1/2 cups (105g) stale breadcrumbs

2 teaspoons grated lime rind

3 green onions, chopped finely

vegetable oil, for deep-frying

sweet chilli sauce

1/2 cup (125ml) mild sweet chilli sauce

1/4 cup (60ml) lime juice

1 clove garlic, crushed

1 tablespoon fish sauce

2 red thai chillies, seeded, chopped finely

Blend or process chicken, capsicum, garlic, coriander, chilli, sauce, egg, breadcrumbs and rind until combined.
Combine chicken mixture with green onion in a medium bowl. Using floured hands, shape tablespoonfuls of chicken mixture into patties.
Deep-fry patties, in batches, in hot oil until browned and cooked through; drain on absorbent paper. Serve with sweet chilli sauce.
Sweet chilli sauce Combine ingredients in small bowl.

MAKES 35
per patty 4.1g fat; 264kJ
on the table in 40 minutes

28 split pea

patties with tomato salad

1 cup (200g) yellow
split peas

3 cups (750ml)
vegetable stock

1/4 cup (25g) packaged
breadcrumbs

1 medium potato
(200g), grated coarsely

1 medium carrot
(120g), grated
coarsely

1/4 cup (35g) sesame
seeds, toasted

1 egg, beaten lightly

2 teaspoons
curry powder

tomato salad

4 medium egg
tomatoes (300g)

4 green onions,
chopped finely

2 tablespoons
shredded fresh mint

1/4 cup (60ml) olive oil

3 teaspoons black
bean sauce

2 tablespoons
lime juice

Combine peas and stock in
large saucepan; simmer,
covered, about 20 minutes
or until peas are very soft and
stock is absorbed. You need
2 cups of the pea mixture.
Combine pea mixture with
remaining ingredients in large
bowl. Using hands, shape
mixture into 12 patties.
Cook patties in large oiled
grill pan (or grill or barbecue)
until browned both sides. Serve
patties with tomato salad.
Tomato salad Cut tomatoes
into wedges; combine with
remaining ingredients in
large bowl.

SERVES 4
per serving 22.2g fat; 1840kJ
on the table in 40 minutes

30 cantonese lamb
patties

1 tablespoon olive oil

1 small white onion (80g), chopped finely

1 tablespoon finely chopped fresh lemon grass

2 cloves garlic, crushed

1 tablespoon grated fresh ginger

1kg minced lamb

3 green onions, chopped finely

1 tablespoon soy sauce

1 tablespoon hoisin sauce

1/4 teaspoon sesame oil

1 egg, beaten lightly

1/2 cup (35g) breadcrumbs

1 1/2 cups (120g) bean sprouts

1/4 cup (60ml) sweet chilli sauce

1 tablespoon water

1 tablespoon lime juice

1 tablespoon finely chopped fresh coriander

Heat olive oil in small saucepan; cook white onion, lemon grass, garlic and ginger, stirring, until onion is soft.
Combine onion mixture in large bowl with lamb, green onion, sauces, sesame oil, egg and breadcrumbs.
Using hands, shape 1/3-cup measures of mixture into patties; cook, in batches, in large heated oiled non-stick frying pan until browned both sides and cooked through. Serve with sprouts and combined remaining ingredients.

SERVES 6
per serving 21.2g fat; 1577kJ
on the table in 40 minutes

fritters with yogurt dip

Besan flour is made from ground chickpeas.

³/₄ cup (110g) besan flour

³/₄ cup (110g) self-raising flour

2 cloves garlic, crushed

1 teaspoon garam masala

1 teaspoon chilli powder

1 teaspoon cumin seeds

1 tablespoon finely chopped fresh coriander

1 cup (250ml) water

1 medium potato (200g), chopped finely

1 small eggplant (230g), chopped finely

1 medium zucchini (120g), chopped finely

250g cauliflower, chopped finely

vegetable oil, for deep-frying

yogurt dip

1 teaspoon cumin seeds

1 cup (280g) yogurt

1 red thai chilli, chopped

¹/₂ teaspoon paprika

2 tablespoons finely chopped fresh mint

1 tablespoon finely chopped fresh coriander

Sift flours into large bowl. Stir in garlic, garam masala, chilli powder, seeds and coriander. Make well in centre; gradually stir in the water, mix to a batter. Stir in vegetables.

Cook heaped tablespoons of mixture, in batches, in hot oil until golden; drain on absorbent paper. Serve with yogurt dip.

Yogurt dip Place seeds in small frying pan, stir over medium heat for about 2 minutes or until fragrant; remove from heat. Combine seeds with remaining ingredients in small bowl; mix well.

MAKES 45
per fritter 1.9g fat; 173kJ
on the table in 40 minutes

32   add a little **bite**

A dollop of concentrated, lip-smacking flavour is all that's necessary to pep up burgers, rösti and fritters. Whether sauce, paste or relish, these recipes fit the bill perfectly.

corn relish and cream

250g jar corn relish

1¼ cups (300g) sour cream

few drops Tabasco sauce

2 tablespoons finely chopped fresh chives

Combine ingredients in medium bowl.

MAKES 2 CUPS (500ml)
per tablespoon 5g fat; 250kJ

cashew, coriander and mint pesto

1¾ cups (275g) raw cashews, toasted

300g bunch fresh coriander

¼ cup firmly packed fresh mint leaves

¼ cup (60ml) lime juice

⅔ cup (160ml) olive oil

Blend or process cashews, coriander, mint and juice until well combined. **With** motor operating, gradually pour in oil; process until thick.

MAKES 2¼ CUPS (560ml)
per tablespoon 18.8g fat; 812kJ

hot and spicy tomato sauce

We used ready-made pesto sauce flavoured with roasted capsicum in this recipe.

1 tablespoon olive oil

1 large white onion (200g), chopped finely

4 medium tomatoes (760g), chopped

1 tablespoon balsamic vinegar

1 teaspoon sugar

½ cup (125ml) red pesto

2 teaspoons sambal oelek

Heat oil in large frying pan, add onion; cook, stirring, until soft.
Add remaining ingredients to pan; simmer, uncovered, about 10 minutes or until tomato is pulpy.

MAKES 2½ CUPS (625ml)
per tablespoon 3.8g fat; 194kJ

sun-dried tomato tapenade

⅓ cup (50g) drained, chopped sun-dried tomatoes

⅔ cup (110g) seedless black olives

1 clove garlic, crushed

2 tablespoons coarsely chopped fresh basil

¼ cup (60ml) olive oil

Blend or process tomato, olives, garlic and basil until smooth.
Add oil gradually in a thin stream, with motor operating; process until smooth.

MAKES ⅔ CUP (160ml)
per tablespoon 7.4g fat; 372kJ

34 rösti with ham
and cherry tomatoes

200g shaved ham

4 large potatoes (1.2kg), grated coarsely

1 egg white, beaten lightly

vegetable oil, for shallow-frying

200g cherry tomatoes

2 green onions, chopped coarsely

Place ham on oven tray; cook in hot oven, uncovered, until browned lightly.
Meanwhile, combine potato and egg white in large bowl; divide into eight portions. Cook rösti, in batches, in hot oil, forming into flat pancake shapes while cooking, until browned both sides and cooked through. Drain on absorbent paper.
Cook tomatoes in small saucepan until just beginning to soften. Serve rösti topped with ham, tomato and onion.

SERVES 4
per serving 37.8g fat; 2412kJ
on the table in 40 minutes

36 trout patties

with pickled ginger

500g fresh trout fillets

1 egg white

1 green onion, chopped finely

2 tablespoons chopped fresh coriander

1 red thai chilli, chopped finely

2 tablespoons cornflour

1 tablespoon peanut oil

2 tablespoons pickled ginger slices

2 tablespoons chervil leaves

Remove skin and bones from trout. Chop trout meat finely; combine trout, egg white, onion, coriander, chilli and cornflour in medium bowl. Using hands, shape mixture into 12 patties.
Heat oil in large non-stick frying pan; cook patties, in batches, until browned both sides and cooked through.
Serve topped with ginger and chervil.

SERVES 4
per serving 9.4g fat; 872kJ
on the table in 40 minutes

600g piece firm tofu

1 clove garlic, crushed

¹/₂ cup (125ml) barbecue sauce

2 tablespoons vegetable oil

1 large red onion (300g), sliced thinly

6 bread rolls

1 baby cos lettuce

2 medium tomatoes (380g), sliced

Cut tofu into 12 slices. Combine tofu, garlic and half of the barbecue sauce in large shallow dish.

Heat half of the oil on a barbecue plate (or in large frying pan); cook onion until soft, remove from barbecue.

Heat remaining oil on barbecue plate; cook tofu until browned both sides and heated through.

Split each roll in half, toast both sides. Top each base with lettuce, tofu, remaining sauce, tomato and onion; top with remaining bread half.

SERVES 6
per serving 15.2g fat; 1607kJ
on the table in 30 minutes

38 crab cakes

2 green onions, chopped finely
1 trimmed celery stick (75g), chopped finely
500g crab meat
2 egg whites, beaten lightly
1 tablespoon finely chopped fresh dill
1 tablespoon worcestershire sauce
1 cup (70g) stale breadcrumbs

soy and honey sauce
½ cup (125ml) soy sauce
2 tablespoons honey

Cook onion and celery in large heated oiled non-stick frying pan until onion is soft.
Combine onion mixture with remaining ingredients in large bowl. Using hands, shape mixture into 12 cakes.
Cook cakes, in batches, in same pan until browned both sides and cooked through.
Serve crab cakes with soy and honey sauce, and green salad, if desired.
Soy and honey sauce Combine ingredients in small bowl.

SERVES 4
per serving 2.2g fat; 918kJ
on the table in 35 minutes

40 ginger, chicken
and lime patties

340g chicken breast fillets, chopped coarsely

1 tablespoon grated lime rind

1 tablespoon grated fresh ginger

2 teaspoons ground cumin

1 egg white

2 green onions, sliced

1/4 cup (35g) plain flour

2 tablespoons vegetable oil

chilli sauce

2 medium red capsicums (400g)

1 medium brown onion (150g), chopped finely

4 red thai chillies, chopped finely

415g can diced tomatoes

1 tablespoon brown sugar

Preheat oven to moderate. Blend or process chicken until finely chopped. Add rind, ginger, cumin, egg white and onion; process until mixture forms a paste. Using floured hands, shape mixture into eight patties. Coat patties in flour; shake away excess.
Heat oil in large non-stick frying pan; cook patties until lightly browned both sides.
Place patties on oven tray; bake, uncovered, in moderate oven about 15 minutes or until cooked through. Serve with chilli sauce and slices of lime, if desired.
Chilli sauce Quarter capsicums, remove and discard seeds and membranes. Roast under grill or in very hot oven, skin-side up, until skin blisters and blackens. Cover capsicum pieces with plastic or paper for 5 minutes; peel away skin, chop pieces finely. Meanwhile, heat oiled medium frying pan; cook onion and chilli, stirring, until onion is soft. Stir in tomato and sugar; simmer, uncovered, 5 minutes, stir in capsicum.

SERVES 4
per serving 14.5g fat; 1256kJ
on the table in 45 minutes

42 smoked salmon

and rösti stacks

200ml crème fraîche

1 tablespoon finely chopped fresh dill

2 tablespoons horseradish cream

1 teaspoon finely grated lemon rind

5 medium pontiac potatoes (1kg)

1 clove garlic, crushed

1/2 teaspoon cracked black pepper

1/4 cup finely chopped fresh chives

1 egg, beaten lightly

1/4 cup (35g) plain flour

vegetable oil, for shallow-frying

16 thin slices (250g) smoked salmon

Combine crème fraîche, dill, horseradish cream and rind in small bowl.

Grate potatoes coarsely, squeeze out excess moisture. Combine potato in large bowl with garlic, pepper, chives, egg and flour; mix well.

Heat oil in medium frying pan; cook 1/4-cup measures of potato mixture, in batches, until browned both sides and crisp. Drain on absorbent paper. Place one rösti on each serving plate, top with two slices salmon and 1 tablespoon crème fraîche mixture; repeat, then finish each stack with a third rösti and remaining crème fraîche mixture.

SERVES 4
per serving 52.3g fat; 3086kJ
on the table in 20 minutes

44 potato lentil patties

1kg potatoes

1/2 cup (100g) red lentils

2 teaspoons olive oil

1 small brown onion (80g), chopped finely

1 clove garlic, crushed

1 egg, beaten lightly

2 tablespoons finely chopped fresh chives

1 tablespoon finely shredded fresh basil

1/3 cup (25g) finely grated parmesan cheese

1/2 cup (125ml) sweet chilli sauce

Preheat oven to moderately hot. Boil, steam or microwave potatoes until tender; drain, mash.

Meanwhile, cook lentils, uncovered, in small saucepan of boiling water for about 8 minutes or until tender. Drain lentils, rinse under cold water; drain.

Heat oil in small non-stick frying pan; cook onion and garlic, stirring, until onion is soft.

Combine potato, lentils, onion mixture, egg and herbs in large bowl. Using hands, shape mixture into 12 patties.

Place patties on baking-paper-lined oven tray; sprinkle with cheese. Bake, uncovered, in moderately hot oven about 30 minutes or until lightly browned; serve with chilli sauce and tomato slices, if desired.

MAKES 12
per patty 2.6g fat; 478kJ
on the table in 55 minutes

400g trim lamb
mini roast

1 tablespoon
harissa

1 tablespoon
lemon juice

2 tablespoons
chopped fresh
coriander root

4 sourdough rolls

1 tablespoon olive oil

1 butter lettuce

2 small tomatoes
(260g), sliced thickly

1/3 cup (95g) yogurt

Combine lamb, harissa, juice and coriander
in small bowl.
Cook lamb on oiled barbecue until browned all
over and cooked as desired. Wrap lamb in foil;
stand for 10 minutes.
Meanwhile, slice each roll in thirds, brush with
oil and cook on barbecue until lightly browned.
Slice lamb and layer between slices of roll,
with lettuce and tomato. Top with yogurt.

SERVES 4
per serving 13.6g fat; 1645kJ
on the table in 35 minutes

46 potato and

sesame rösti

1 tablespoon vegetable oil
1 small red onion (100g), chopped finely
3 medium potatoes (600g)
1/3 cup (50g) sesame seeds, toasted
1 tablespoon cornflour
1/4 cup (60ml) vegetable oil, extra

sauce
1 teaspoon cornflour
2 tablespoons water
1/3 cup (80ml) soy sauce
1/4 cup (60ml) rice vinegar
2 teaspoons sesame oil

Heat oil in small frying pan; cook onion, stirring, until soft. Remove from heat.
Coarsely grate potatoes. Combine onion, potato, seeds and cornflour in large bowl.
Heat extra oil in large non-stick frying pan; cook 1/4-cup measures of potato mixture until browned both sides and crisp. Drain on absorbent paper.
Serve potato cakes with sauce.
Sauce Blend cornflour and the water in small saucepan; stir in remaining ingredients. Stir over heat until mixture boils and thickens slightly.

SERVES 4
per serving 27.8g fat; 1606kJ
on the table in 45 minutes

48 crisp corn and
prawn fritters

Combine onion, celery, garlic, corn and capsicum in large bowl.

Blend or process eggs, garam masala, prawn and chilli until smooth. Stir egg mixture, flour and baking powder into vegetable mixture.

Heat oil in large non-stick frying pan, add rounded tablespoons of mixture; flatten, then cook until golden brown. Drain on absorbent paper. Serve with sauce.

Sauce Stir flour in small saucepan over low heat until lightly browned. Add sugar; stir over low heat until sugar begins to dissolve. Gradually add the water; stir over high heat until mixture boils and thickens, stir in sauce.

MAKES 10
per fritter 6.1g fat; 402kJ
on the table in 35 minutes

4 green onions, chopped

1 trimmed stick celery (75g), chopped finely

1 clove garlic, crushed

130g can corn kernels, rinsed, drained

1 medium green capsicum (200g), chopped finely

2 eggs

1/2 teaspoon garam masala

100g large uncooked prawns, shelled, deveined

2 red thai chillies, seeded, chopped finely

2 tablespoons plain flour

2 teaspoons baking powder

vegetable oil, for shallow-frying

sauce

1 tablespoon plain flour

3 teaspoons brown sugar

1/2 cup (125ml) water

11/2 tablespoons soy sauce

burgers

8 medium tomatoes
(1.5kg)

2 teaspoons
balsamic vinegar

$1/4$ cup (60ml) olive oil

1.5kg minced beef

2 teaspoons finely
grated lemon rind

3 cloves garlic, crushed

1 tablespoon coarsely
chopped fresh oregano

1 loaf ciabatta

1 clove garlic,
crushed, extra

200g fetta, crumbled

100g baby rocket leaves

Preheat oven to hot. Halve tomatoes; cut each half into three wedges. Place wedges on oiled oven tray; drizzle with combined vinegar and 1 tablespoon of the oil. Roast, uncovered, in hot oven about 25 minutes.

Meanwhile, combine beef, rind, garlic and oregano in large bowl; shape mixture into eight patties. Cook patties, in batches, on heated oiled grill plate (or grill or barbecue) until browned both sides and cooked through.

Cut bread into 16 slices, brush with combined remaining oil and extra garlic; cook bread, in batches, on same heated oiled grill plate until browned both sides.

Sandwich patties, fetta, tomato and rocket between bread pieces.

SERVES 8
per serving 34.8g fat; 2792kJ
on the table in 40 minutes

50 corned beef
hash with poached eggs

1 medium brown onion (150g), chopped finely

3 medium potatoes (600g), grated coarsely

500g cooked corned beef, shredded

2 tablespoons finely chopped fresh flat-leaf parsley

2 tablespoons plain flour

2 eggs, beaten lightly

1 tablespoon vegetable oil

4 eggs, extra

1 tablespoon shredded fresh basil

Combine onion, potato, beef, parsley, flour and egg in large bowl. Using hands, shape mixture into four patties.

Heat oil in large non-stick frying pan; cook patties until browned both sides and cooked through.

Break extra eggs into greased egg rings in barely simmering water; poach eggs until cooked as desired. Carefully lift rings away from eggs; lift eggs from water, drain.

Serve hash patties topped with poached eggs; top with basil.

SERVES 2

per serving 37.8g fat; 3387kJ

on the table in 20 minutes

52 lamb patties with
tomato and oregano salsa

800g minced lamb

1/2 cup (60g) seeded black olives, chopped finely

100g pancetta, chopped finely

2 tablespoons finely chopped fresh oregano

1 tablespoon dijon mustard

1 tablespoon tomato paste

1 teaspoon cracked black pepper

tomato and oregano salsa

1 medium avocado (250g), chopped finely

2 medium tomatoes (380g), chopped finely

2 teaspoons finely chopped fresh oregano

1 tablespoon lemon juice

1 tablespoon olive oil

1 teaspoon balsamic vinegar

Combine ingredients in large bowl; using hands, shape mixture into eight patties.
Cook patties, in batches, on heated oiled grill plate (or grill or barbecue) until browned both sides and cooked through; serve with tomato and oregano salsa.
Tomato and oregano salsa Combine ingredients in small bowl.

SERVES 4
per serving 37.9g fat; 2332kJ
on the table in 30 minutes

rice and zucchini patties

You will need to cook about ¾ cup (150g) of brown rice for this recipe.

1½ cups cooked brown rice

3 medium green zucchini (300g), grated coarsely

1 medium brown onion (150g), chopped finely

2 tablespoons finely chopped fresh flat-leaf parsley

2 eggs, beaten lightly

1 cup (70g) stale breadcrumbs

130g can creamed corn

¼ cup (60ml) olive oil

Combine rice, zucchini, onion, parsley, egg, breadcrumbs and corn in large bowl. Using hands, shape mixture into 12 patties.
Heat oil in large frying pan. Cook patties until browned both sides and heated through; drain on absorbent paper.

SERVES 4
per patty 18.3g fat; 1608kJ
on the table in 30 minutes

54 chicken burger

with avocado cream

800g minced chicken

2 bacon rashers, chopped finely

1/3 cup (25g) grated parmesan cheese

3 green onions, chopped finely

1 egg, beaten lightly

1/2 cup (50g) packaged breadcrumbs

1 tablespoon vegetable oil

20cm-square focaccia

1 cup snow pea sprouts

2 small tomatoes (260g), sliced

1 medium carrot (120g), thinly sliced

avocado cream

1 medium avocado (250g), chopped

125g packaged cream cheese, softened

1 tablespoon lemon juice

Combine chicken, bacon, cheese, onion, egg and breadcrumbs in medium bowl. Using hands, shape mixture into four patties.

Heat oil in medium non-stick frying pan; cook patties until browned both sides and cooked through.

Cut focaccia into four pieces; split each in half, toast cut surfaces. Top bases with sprouts, patties, avocado cream, tomato and carrot; replace tops.

Avocado cream Combine ingredients in bowl; mash with a fork until well combined.

SERVES 4
per serving 53.4g fat; 3441kJ
on the table in 35 minutes

56 carrot and dill rösti

1/4 cup (60g) light sour cream

1 teaspoon ground cumin

1 tablespoon finely chopped fresh dill

5 medium carrots (600g), grated coarsely

1 egg, beaten lightly

1 egg white, beaten lightly

1/3 cup (50g) plain flour

Combine sour cream, cumin and dill in small bowl.

Combine carrot, egg, egg white and flour in large bowl. Cook 1/4-cup measures of carrot mixture, in batches, on heated oiled barbecue plate until rösti are browned both sides and cooked through; drain on absorbent paper.

Serve rösti with sour cream mixture.

SERVES 4
per serving 4.8g fat; 574kJ
on the table in 20 minutes

5 large zucchini (750g), grated coarsely

1 medium white onion (150g), chopped finely

½ cup (75g) plain flour

3 eggs, beaten lightly

1 tablespoon chopped fresh oregano

1 tablespoon chopped fresh basil

1 tablespoon chopped fresh flat-leaf parsley

vegetable oil, for shallow-frying

Combine zucchini, onion, flour, egg and herbs in medium bowl.

Cook ¼-cup measures of zucchini mixture, in batches, in hot oil until fritters are browned both sides and cooked through; drain on absorbent paper.

MAKES 10
per fritter 13.3g fat; 686kJ
on the table in 25 minutes

58 kumara

ginger fritters

1 tablespoon
vegetable oil

1 small white onion
(80g), chopped finely

1 medium zucchini
(120g), grated
coarsely

2 teaspoons grated
fresh ginger

2 teaspoons mild
sweet chilli sauce

1 medium kumara
(400g), grated
coarsely

1 tablespoon
finely chopped
fresh coriander

2 eggs, beaten lightly

1/3 cup (50g) plain flour

2 tablespoons
sesame seeds

vegetable oil,
for deep-frying

**chilli coriander
yogurt**

1/2 cup (140g) yogurt

1 tablespoon chopped
fresh coriander

2 teaspoons mild
sweet chilli sauce

Heat oil in large frying pan; cook onion, zucchini, ginger and sauce, stirring, until onion is soft. Combine onion mixture, kumara, coriander, egg, flour and seeds in large bowl.
Cook tablespoons of mixture in hot oil until browned and cooked through; drain on absorbent paper.
Serve warm fritters with chilli coriander yogurt.
Chilli coriander yogurt Combine ingredients in small bowl.

MAKES 20
per fritter 6.5g fat; 369kJ
on the table in 35 minutes

glossary

bacon rashers also known as slices of bacon, made from cured, smoked pork.

baking powder a raising agent consisting mainly of two parts cream of tartar to one part bicarbonate of soda (baking soda).

beetroot also known as red beets; firm, round root vegetable.

black bean sauce a Chinese sauce made from fermented soy beans, spices, water and wheat flour.

breadcrumbs
packaged: crunchy, fine-textured white breadcrumbs; purchase at supermarkets.
stale: one- or two-day-old bread made into crumbs by grating, blending or processing.

butter use salted or unsalted (sweet) butter; 125g is equal to one stick of butter.

capsicum also known as pepper or bell pepper.

cheese
cream: commonly known as Philadelphia or Philly, a soft cow-milk cheese.
fetta: a white, crumbly, salty cheese most commonly made from cow milk.
parmesan: a sharp-tasting, dry, hard cheese. We used fresh parmesan cheese.
ricotta: a sweet, moist, fresh curd cheese.

chillies available in many different types and sizes. Use rubber gloves when seeding and chopping fresh chillies as they can burn your skin. Removing seeds and membranes lessens the heat level.

choy sum also known as flowering bok choy, flowering white cabbage or chinese flowering cabbage. The stems, leaves and yellow flowers are used.

ciabatta a crisp-crusted white Italian bread.

cornflour also known as cornstarch; used as a thickening agent.

cream, sour a thick, commercially cultured soured cream.

crème fraîche mature, fermented cream that has a tangy flavour and rich, velvety texture.

eggplant also known as aubergine.

fennel also known as finocchio or anise.

flour
besan: a flour made from ground chickpeas.
plain: all-purpose flour, made from wheat.
self-raising: plain flour sifted with baking powder in the proportion of 1 cup flour to 2 teaspoons baking powder.

ginger
fresh: also known as green or root ginger.
ground: also known as powdered ginger; cannot be substituted for fresh ginger.
pink pickled: available in jars from Asian grocery stores; pickled, paper-thin shavings of ginger in a mixture of vinegar, sugar and natural colouring.

harissa paste or sauce made from dried red chillies, garlic, oil and caraway seeds.

hoisin sauce a thick, sweet and spicy paste made from fermented, salted soy beans, onions and garlic.

horseradish cream a creamy prepared paste of grated horseradish, vinegar, oil and sugar.

jalapeños, pickled sold finely chopped or whole, bottled in vinegar.

kumara orange-fleshed sweet potato often confused with yam.

lentils available in red, brown and yellow; dried pulses often identified by and named after their colour.

minced meat also known as ground meat, as in beef, pork, lamb, chicken and veal.

mustard, dijon pale brown, fairly mild, distinctively flavoured French mustard.

oil
olive: made from ripened olives. Extra virgin and virgin are the best quality; extra light or light refers to the taste not the fat content of oil.
peanut: pressed from ground peanuts; most commonly used oil in Asian cooking because of its high smoke point.
sesame: made from roasted, crushed white sesame seeds; used to give flavour, rather than as a cooking medium.
vegetable: any of a number of oils sourced from plants rather than animal fat.

onion
green: also known as scallion or (incorrectly) shallot; an immature onion picked before the bulb has formed, having a long, bright-green edible stalk.
red: also known as spanish, red spanish or bermuda onion; a sweet-flavoured, large, purple-red onion.

pancetta an Italian, spiced, salt-cured pork roll, usually cut from the belly.

pide also known as turkish bread; comes in long, flat loaves as well as individual rounds. Made from wheat flour and sprinkled with sesame or black onion seeds.

rice vermicelli also known as rice-flour or rice-stick noodles; made from ground rice. Sold dried; best either deep-fried, or soaked then used in a stir-fry or soup.

rice vinegar colourless vinegar made from fermented rice, and flavoured with sugar and salt.

saffron available in threads or ground form; imparts a yellow-orange colour to food once infused.

sambal oelek (also ulek or olek) a salty paste made from chillies and vinegar.

stock 1 cup (250ml) stock equals 1 cup (250ml) water plus 1 crumbled stock cube or 1 teaspoon stock powder.

sweet chilli sauce a relatively mild, Thai-style sauce made from red chillies, sugar, garlic and vinegar.

yellow split peas also known as field peas. Green or yellow pulse grown specially for drying; split in half along a centre seam.

yogurt we used plain, unflavoured yogurt, unless otherwise specified.

zucchini also known as courgette.

facts and figures 63

These conversions are approximate only, but the difference between an exact and the approximate conversion of various liquid and dry measures is minimal and will not affect your cooking results.

Measuring equipment

The difference between one country's measuring cups and another's is, at most, within a 2 or 3 teaspoon variance. (For the record, 1 Australian metric measuring cup holds approximately 250ml.) The most accurate way of measuring dry ingredients is to weigh them. For liquids, use a clear glass or plastic jug having metric markings.

Note: NZ, Canada, USA and UK all use 15ml tablespoons. Australian tablespoons measure 20ml.
All cup and spoon measurements are level.

How to measure

When using graduated measuring cups, shake dry ingredients loosely into the appropriate cup. Do not tap the cup on a bench or tightly pack the ingredients unless directed to do so. Level the top of measuring cups and measuring spoons with a knife. When measuring liquids, place a clear glass or plastic jug having metric markings on a flat surface to check accuracy at eye level.

Dry Measures

metric	imperial
15g	1/2oz
30g	1oz
60g	2oz
90g	3oz
125g	4oz (1/4lb)
155g	5oz
185g	6oz
220g	7oz
250g	8oz (1/2lb)
280g	9oz
315g	10oz
345g	11oz
375g	12oz (3/4lb)
410g	13oz
440g	14oz
470g	15oz
500g	16oz (1lb)
750g	24oz (11/2lb)
1kg	32oz (2lb)

We use large eggs having an average weight of 60g.

Liquid Measures

metric	imperial
30ml	1 fluid oz
60ml	2 fluid oz
100ml	3 fluid oz
125ml	4 fluid oz
150ml	5 fluid oz (1/4 pint/1 gill)
190ml	6 fluid oz
250ml (1cup)	8 fluid oz
300ml	10 fluid oz (1/2 pint)
500ml	16 fluid oz
600ml	20 fluid oz (1 pint)
1000ml (1litre)	13/4 pints

Oven Temperatures

These oven temperatures are only a guide.
Always check the manufacturer's manual.

	°C (Celsius)	°F (Fahrenheit)	Gas Mark
Very slow	120	250	1
Slow	150	300	2
Moderately slow	160	325	3
Moderate	180 –190	350 – 375	4
Moderately hot	200 – 210	400 – 425	5
Hot	220 – 230	450 – 475	6
Very hot	240 – 250	500 – 525	7

Helpful Measures

metric	imperial
3mm	1/8in
6mm	1/4in
1cm	1/2in
2cm	3/4in
2.5cm	1in
6cm	21/2in
8cm	3in
20cm	8in
23cm	9in
25cm	10in
30cm	12in (1ft)

at your fingertips

These elegant slipcovers store up to 10 mini books and make the books instantly accessible.

And the metric measuring cups and spoons make following our recipes a piece of cake.

Book Holder
Australia and overseas:
$A8.95 (incl. GST).

Metric Measuring Set
Australia: $6.50 (incl. GST).
New Zealand: $A8.00.
Elsewhere: $A9.95.
Prices include postage
and handling.
This offer is available
in all countries.

Mail or fax Photocopy and complete the coupon below and post to ACP Books Reader Offer, ACP Publishing, GPO Box 4967, Sydney NSW 2001, or fax to (02) 9267 4967.

Phone Have your credit card details ready, then phone 136 116 (Mon-Fri, 8.00am - 6.00pm; Sat 8.00am - 6.00pm).

Australian residents We accept the credit cards listed on the coupon, money orders and cheques.

Overseas residents We accept the credit cards listed on the coupon, drafts in $A drawn on an Australian bank, and also British, New Zealand and U.S. cheques in the currency of the country of issue.

Photocopy and complete the coupon below

☐ **Book holder** ☐ **Metric measuring set**
Please indicate number(s) required.

Mr/Mrs/Ms _____

Address _____

_____

Postcode _____ Country _____

Phone: Business hours ( ) _____

I enclose my cheque/money order for $_____ payable to ACP Publishing

OR: please charge $ _____ to my: ☐ Bankcard ☐ Visa

☐ Amex ☐ MasterCard ☐ Diners Club Expiry Date ___/___

Cardholder's signature _____

Please allow up to 30 days for delivery within Australia.
Allow up to 6 weeks for overseas deliveries. Both offers expire 31/12/02.
HLMBRF02

Food director Pamela Clark
Food editor Louise Patniotis

ACP BOOKS STAFF
Editorial director Susan Tomnay
Senior editor Julie Collard
Concept design Jackie Richards
Designer Caryl Wiggins
Publishing manager (sales) Jennifer McDon
Publishing manager (rights & new titles)
Jane Hazell
Assistant brand manager Donna Gianniotis
Production manager Carol Currie

Publisher Sue Wannan
Group publisher Jill Baker
Chief executive officer John Alexander

Produced by ACP Books, Sydney.

Colour separations by
ACP Colour Graphics Pty Ltd, Sydney.
Printing by Dai Nippon Printing in Hong Kong

Published by ACP Publishing Pty Limited,
54 Park St, Sydney; GPO Box 4088, Sydney,
NSW 1028. Ph: (02) 9282 8618
Fax: (02) 9267 9438.
acpbooks@acp.com.au
www.acpbooks.com.au

To order books, phone 136 116.
Send recipe enquiries to
Recipeenquiries@acp.com.au

Australia Distributed by Network Services,
GPO Box 4088, Sydney, NSW 1028.
Ph: (02) 9282 8777 Fax: (02) 9264 3278.

United Kingdom Distributed by Australian
Consolidated Press (UK), Moulton Park Busin
Centre, Red House Road, Moulton Park,
Northampton, NN3 6AQ. Ph: (01604) 497 531
Fax: (01604) 497 533 acpukltd@aol.com

Canada Distributed by Whitecap Books Ltd,
351 Lynn Ave, North Vancouver, BC, V7J 2C4
Ph: (604) 980 9852.

New Zealand Distributed by Netlink Distributi
Company, Level 4, 23 Hargreaves St,
College Hill, Auckland 1, Ph: (9) 302 7616.

South Africa Distributed by
PSD Promotions (Pty) Ltd, PO Box 1175,
Isando 1600, SA, Ph: (011) 392 6065.

Clark, Pamela.
Burgers, rösti & fritters.

Includes index.
ISBN 1 86396 274 3

1. Cookery. 2. Hamburgers. 3. Cookery (Potat
I. Title: Australian Women's Weekly.
(Series: Australian Women's Weekly
Make it Tonight mini series).

641.5

© ACP Publishing Pty Limited 2002
ABN 18 053 273 546

Cover: Vegetarian burger, page 37.
Stylist: Georgina Dolling
Photographer: Joe Filshie
Back cover: Crispy pumpkin cakes, page 16